ZION
National Park

by Ruth Radlauer

Photographs by
Ed and Ruth Radlauer

Design and map by Rolf Zillmer

AN ELK GROVE BOOK

 CHILDRENS PRESS, CHICAGO

With special thanks to the naturalists
who give Zion National Park more meaning.

Photo credits:
    Capitol Reef National Park, p. 47
    Glacier National Park, p. 35 (beaver)
    Rolf Zillmer, pages 37 (bottom)
    and 47 (Arches and Bryce)
    Zion National Park, Allen Hagood, p. 13 (top)

Cover: Hoodoo, East Side Of Zion National Park

Library of Congress Cataloging in Publication Data

Radlauer, Ruth Shaw.
  Zion National Park.

  (Parks for people)
  ''An Elk Grove book.''
  SUMMARY: Describes the rock formations, wildlife,
vegetation, and hiking trails found in Utah's Zion
National Park.
  1. Zion National Park—Juvenile literature.
[1. Zion National Park. 2. National parks and
reserves] I. Radlauer, Edward. II. Zillmer, Rolf.
III. Title.
F832.Z8R33   917.92'48   78-4028
ISBN 0-516-07497-0

1 2 3 4 5 6 7 8 9 10 11 12 13 14 15 R 84 83 82 81 80 79 78

Contents

What is Zion National Park?

Zion National Park is a place of many surprises. Everywhere you look there is a new sight, a new sound, another surprise. Towering rocks and cliffs stand in the morning sun and cast giant shadows on a canyon far below.

In spring, many different kinds of flowers nod in cool breezes. Then Zion is the sweet smell of shooting stars and columbines. Or it may be the sharp scent of sage and a breath of crisp, clean air.

Zion is the sight of a black raven soaring over the red rocks of Kolob Canyons and the feel of hairy bark on a juniper tree.

Zion National Park is the sound of your footsteps echoing against narrow canyon walls on the trail to Angels Landing. It's the squeak of a leather saddle when you ride a horse on Zion trails. If you are very quiet when you stop on a canyon hike, Zion is the sound of grains of sand falling on dry leaves. Grain by grain, the canyon walls are falling away. Does it surprise you that these rocks may not even be here a million years from now?

ion National Park

One Way To Cross A River

Cliff Columbine

Your Trip to Zion

A good way to make a trip to a national park more interesting is to read about it before you go there. Write the superintendent for a free map and list of books and pamphlets about the park. Zion's address is Springdale, Utah 84767. The map tells about park features and campgrounds. The books may be in your library, or you can buy them from the Zion Natural History Association at the park.

As you read, you find out this is a wonderful hiker's park. You can stroll a short way or trudge as far as you like into side canyons. With a free permit, you can spend a few days backpacking in the wilderness. So, of course, you'll take good hiking boots, a bottle or canteen, and clothes to keep you warm or let you be cool. If you like to take pictures, you'll need lots of film, and birdwatchers enjoy binoculars.

From Salt Lake City to the north or from Las Vegas, Nevada, to the south, Interstate 15 leads to Utah Routes 9 and 17, the turnoffs to Zion Park. People also come to the park from the east on Highway 89 to Utah 9 at Mount Carmel Junction.

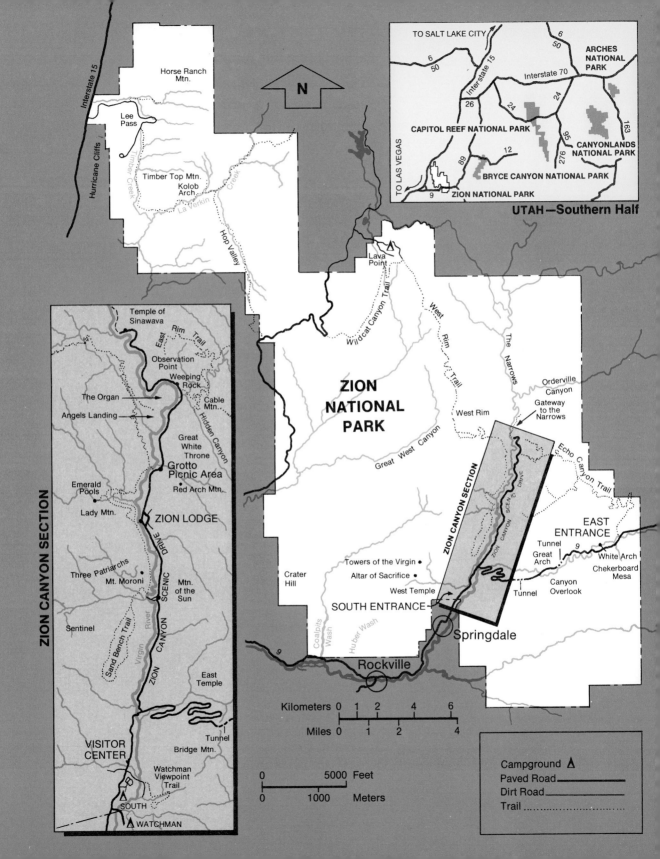

N

UTAH—Southern Half

TO SALT LAKE CITY

ARCHES
NATIONAL
PARK

Interstate 70

CAPITOL REEF NATIONAL PARK

CANYONLANDS
NATIONAL PARK

TO LAS VEGAS

BRYCE CANYON NATIONAL PARK

ZION NATIONAL PARK

Interstate 15

Horse Ranch Mtn.

Lee Pass

Timber Creek

Timber Top Mtn.
Kolob Arch

La Verkin

Hurricane Cliffs

Hop Valley

Lava Point

Wildcat Canyon Trail

West Rim Trail

The Narrows

**ZION
NATIONAL
PARK**

West Rim

Orderville Canyon

Gateway to the Narrows

Great West Canyon

Echo Canyon Trail

EAST
ENTRANCE

Crater Hill

Towers of the Virgin

Altar of Sacrifice

West Temple

SOUTH ENTRANCE

Coalpits Wash

Huber Wash

9

Rockville

Springdale

Tunnel
Great Arch

9

Canyon Overlook

Tunnel

White Arch

Chekerboard Mesa

ZION CANYON SECTION

Kilometers 0   1   2   4   6

Miles 0   1   2   4

Campground ⋀
Paved Road
Dirt Road
Trail

ZION CANYON SECTION

Temple of Sinawava

East Rim Trail

Observation Point

Weeping Rock

The Organ

Angels Landing

Cable Mtn.

Hidden Canyon

Great White Throne

Grotto Picnic Area

Red Arch Mtn.

Emerald Pools

Lady Mtn.

ZION LODGE

Three Patriarchs

Mt. Moroni

Mtn. of the Sun

Sentinel

Sand Bench Trail

Virgin River

ZION CANYON SCENIC DRIVE

East Temple

Tunnel

Bridge Mtn.

VISITOR CENTER

Watchman Viewpoint Trail

SOUTH

WATCHMAN

0   5000 Feet

0   1000 Meters

Layers of Time

The biggest surprise in Zion is the size of the rocks and the way they were formed. Scientists tell us that millions of years ago, the areas of southern Utah and northern Arizona were part of a huge basin that sank very slowly. Water flowed into the basin and formed a shallow sea.

Rivers carried sand, silt, and mud from higher places into the water where they settled as layers of *sediments* on the sea bottom. Slowly, the sediments packed together into layers of *sedimentary rock.*

Then the land rose very slowly. The water drained away, and for the next ten million years, winds brought sand from the west. Swirling and flying, the sand piled into hills, or dunes. As the winds changed directions, they shifted the dunes first one way, then the other.

Later, water covered the area again, and a layer of limestone was laid down. When minerals from the limestone seeped down into the layer of sand underneath it, they cemented the grains of sand together. Beneath the limestone, the ancient dunes became sandstone.

Checkerboard Mesa—Ancient Dunes Turned To Stone

Markagunt Plateau

How did the rocks of Zion turn from underground masses of sandstone into the "sculptures" we see today? About 60 million years ago, the Colorado Plateau began to rise. The earth's crust over southern Utah and northern Arizona broke into huge blocks many kilometers across. Zion sits on one of these blocks known as the Markagunt Plateau. When the plateau tilted, it formed a cliff along the break, or fault, on its western edge.

If you travel to the Kolob Canyons in the north end of Zion, you can see part of this fault, the Hurricane Cliffs.

When the Markagunt Plateau tilted, its streams ran faster. The rushing water carved deep channels into the layers of rock. As it tore away huge rocks and ground them up, the water gained power. This torrent of water ripped away some of the sedimentary layers and uncovered the ancient rock we call Navajo Sandstone.

Then wind, rain, snow, and ice slowly wore away, or eroded, the rock and created Zion Canyon as we see it today.

Timber Top Mountain and Shuntavi Butte ▶

Nature's Sculptors

The cutting of Zion Canyon has gone on from time to time for about one million years. Today the river is still cutting into Navajo Sandstone in the upper parts of the canyon. Downstream, the Virgin River has cut all the way through the sandstone to the formation beneath it. The river uncovered the sedimentary layer of shale in the Kayenta Formation.

Besides the river, other forces have been at work. For thousands of years, movements within the earth have made its crust rise and fall. In Zion, this earth movement cracked the Navajo Sandstone. Large cracks, known as joints, weakened the rock.

Rain and snow fall on the sandstone and seep down through it. But when the water reaches Kayenta shale, it cannot flow on through. Instead, the water flows outward in seeps and springs. As water carries away the loose shale, it takes away the base on which the rock stands. Already weakened by joints, or cracks, the walls of Zion fall.

All these forces have worked as nature's sculptors, cutting and chipping away at the Navajo Sandstone.

Virgin River From Angels Landing Trail

Arches

The "sculptures" in Zion take different shapes. In places, a chunk, such as the Pulpit in the Temple of Sinawava, stands free. In other places, where the Kayenta shale washes away, a chunk falls. Then the mountain is left with a new steep cliff, a straight-sided niche, or a hollowed arch of stone.

Sometimes these arches are eroded into free-standing ones like the arch high on Bridge Mountain. You can see the free-standing Kolob Arch at the end of a 10½-kilometer hike into the Kolob Canyons area.

But most arches in Zion are blind, like the White Arch on the east side or the one in the face of Red Arch Mountain.

What will happen if this canyon-cutting process goes on for another million years? Could these towers crumble away to sand and become part of a desert once again? Maybe you should hurry to Zion National Park while its giant sculptures still stand like statues in a gallery of nature's artwork.

Kolob Arch

White Arch

Gallery Guides

Zion is like a big art show, an immense art gallery. To make the most of your stay here, go first to the Visitor Center. Here you'll see a relief map of the park and exhibits that explain the history, geology, plants, and animals of Zion.

Park naturalists are there to answer your questions and give you the printed schedule of walks and talks. They even have *Zion Photography Hints,* a map that shows when and where to take the best pictures. The Visitor Center is the place to plan your hikes and decide which evening programs you want to attend.

From the Center, it's a short way to Zion Canyon Scenic Drive. Along this road are turnouts where you can stop to look up at this natural art gallery. Signs tell the names of the "sculptures": The Three Patriarchs, Angels Landing, and others. At the end of the road is the Temple of Sinawava and Gateway to the Narrows Trail.

But there is more to see than huge rocks. Be sure to look around you at the small beauties of Zion. Don't miss a swallowtail butterfly or a hidden cactus garden.

hree Patriarchs

Swallowtail Butterfly

Cactus On A Sandstone Ledge

Petrified Wood

A surprise awaits you near the Visitor Center. It's a petrified log brought here from another part of Zion National Park.

At the end of Huber Wash are some more petrified logs. They're sticking out of a rock wall where they were buried long before this region was covered by a shallow sea. The trees were carried here from far away by rivers and streams. As sediments washed over them, the grain of the wood filled with silica, a mineral found in sand. Bit by bit, silica replaced the wood cells of the trees, and they changed from wood to stone, or petrified wood.

While this was happening, a layer called the Chinle was forming. Later, the Chinle Formation was covered by another layer of sediments that make up the Moenave Formation. Then the Kayenta and other formations collected on top of those.

In the ages that followed, erosion uncovered the Chinle Formation along the Huber and Coalpits Washes. Now you can see the logs that have been buried for millions of years!

Petrified Wood—Chinle Formation, Huber Wash

Hoodoos

Your biggest Zion surprise may be the hoodoos. Most of these strange Navajo Sandstone "sculptures" are on the east side of the park. Very different from the cliffs and towers of Zion Canyon, a hoodoo may look to you like a stack of stone pancakes.

A hoodoo is a column of rock. The hoodoos in Zion have been formed partly because of iron "caps."

Rocks containing a lot of iron sit on sandstone and form a cap, or roof, over the stone. Water cannot seep through the iron into the sandstone.

But water *can* seep into and soften nearby sandstone *without* iron caps. The softened stone washes away, while the sandstone beneath the iron caps withstands some of the forces of erosion.

Be sure to get out of your car and hike among the hoodoos. No one has named them, so maybe you can. What would you call the one that looks like a fat, wrinkled king in a black hat? Which one will be the Dinosaur's Birthday Cake?

Hoodoo With Iron Cap ▶

Anasazi

The first people to see Zion country were probably the Anasazi, or "ancient ones." Between A.D. 1 and 450, these early Basketmakers lived in pit houses and hunted roots, berries, and animals to eat.

As time went on the Anasazi learned to plant corn, squash, and beans. They made clay pots for cooking and stored food for the winter. In the shelter of overhanging rocks, or alcoves, they built granaries. These were round food storage bins made of rocks.

If you look carefully at the alcove above the lower Emerald Pools Trail, you may see a granary. Another sits in an arch across the road from the overlook for the Great White Throne.

The Anasazi left other signs of their stay. They left "picture writing," or petroglyphs, carved on a big slab of rock near the Visitor Center.

In some side canyons on the eastern side of the park, you may find more petroglyphs. What story do you think an "ancient one" was carving in the rock so many years ago?

ranary In An Arch

Petroglyph—Side Canyon

Zion's Many Names

Another group, the Fremont people, lived in the north part of Zion, but they also left in the 1200s. No one is sure why, but some think a very long drought may have driven them away.

Many years later, a wandering tribe, the Paiutes, hunted on plateaus around the Virgin River. They called the river "Pahroos," meaning "muddy, churning water."

The Paiutes seem to have feared the narrow canyon. They called it "loogoon," or arrow quiver, because "one must go out the way one goes in."

Mukuntuweap was the Indian name for this area when early settlers came. But a group of Mormon farmers wanted a new name for it. Since they felt they'd found safety and rest, they called it Zion. In the Bible, Zion was the perfect homeland.

The area became Mukuntuweap National Monument in 1909. Zion was established as a national park in 1919.

But it was in 1916 that many of the rocks were named by a Methodist minister. Of one, he wrote, "I have looked for this mountain all my life, but never expected to find it in this world. It is the Great White Throne."

Great White Throne

Hot and Dry

Zion National Park has many different elevations, different soils, and changing weather conditions. Many spots are hot and dry. To be able to live in these places, some plants and animals have adapted, or changed. They can live in heat with very little water.

When it's very hot, animals like the horned lizard dart from shade to shade or dig down into cooler layers of soil. Mice and other rodents stay in moist burrows. A kangaroo rat's body can make its own water from seeds, and lizards get water from moist food.

The cactus stores water in its plump stems and pads. A leathery, thick skin protects it from drying out. Cacti have widespread, shallow roots that soak up water as soon as dew or rain falls.

Three groups of cacti grow in Zion. The hedgehog type has clumps of parts shaped like barrels. The cholla group has branching, tubelike joints. The most common cactus in Zion is the prickly pear, which has flattened, oval parts. Watch for its yellow or purplish red blooms in sunny spots along trails and roads.

orned Lizard

Prickly Pear Cactus

Zion Slopes

You will see plants of the hot, dry zones if you hike up Huber and Coalpits Washes. From there you can also see the plants of higher Zion slopes.

Yucca, juniper, and pinyon pines dot the slopes. There's lots of sun, but little water, so these plants are spaced well apart. Hiking the Watchman Trail, you can look closely at junipers and pinyons.

Juniper leaves are like green scales that hug every twig. Little moisture can escape from these hard, waxy leaves. A juniper also has a long taproot that reaches deep for water.

Pinyon or nut pines are low and bushy compared with the ponderosa pines growing at higher elevations. Pinyon cones hold big seeds that both squirrels and people find sweet and juicy.

The upper half of the Watchman Trail goes through a forest of these trees. Among the many birds that nest here in spring and summer are mourning doves, black-chinned hummingbirds, and black-headed grosbeaks.

uniper

Cool and Wet

Did you ever see a big rock cry? You will if you take the Emerald Pools hike or the short walk to Weeping Rock. What makes the "tears" that stream down the faces of some Zion cliffs?

Navajo Sandstone is porous. It has billions of open spaces between its grains of sand. Rain and melted snow can seep down through this rock. But when the water reaches the *non*porous shale of the Kayenta Formation, it can no longer flow downward. It flows outward. In some places, water makes a spring. In other spots, the water drops like tears from overhanging rocks.

But no one cries along with the rocks. The "tears" keep the ground soft and wet, so golden and cliff columbines, monkey flowers, and shooting stars can add color to the canyon.

The seeps and springs flow down to join the Virgin River. The soil along the river is a good place for cottonwoods, box elders, and velvet ash trees to take root. These trees are called deciduous, meaning they lose their leaves every year.

Do Rocks Cry?

Deciduous Trees By The Virgin River

Golden Columbine

Evergreens

Deciduous trees have wide leaves that drop once a year. Evergreen leaves stay green all year.

Some evergreens, like the shrub manzanita, have wide leaves. Others, such as pines and firs, have needles. Evergreens with needles usually form their seeds in cones. They're called conifers.

In Zion, many conifers grow at low elevations in cool, shaded side canyons. Most of these are white and Douglas firs, too small to make good lumber. Early settlers wished they could get the tall ponderosa pines down from the high canyon rims to use for building. But the pines may as well have been on the planet Jupiter.

Then, in 1900, a young man began to experiment with wires and pulleys. In about a year, he had made a cable to lower shingles and barrel staves from the rim to the floor of the canyon. Soon he built a sawmill, and for about 20 years, the people of the valley built with lumber brought down from Cable Mountain.

Hanging Valley—Kolob Canyon

Signs of Animals

If you are an animal watcher, you know how to catch a look at wildlife in a national park.

When you walk quietly on the trails, you will see lizards, hummingbirds, and chipmunks. But Zion has some animals few people see: the gray fox, ringtail cat, bank beaver, and others. During the day they stay out of the heat, hidden from other animals and people.

Still, you may see some signs of animals. The bank beaver leaves many fallen trees. With its sharp front teeth, this giant rodent chews at tree trunks, harvesting a supply of building materials and food.

Because the Virgin River floods so often, the beaver cannot build dams and lodges like those of the pond beaver. Zion's beaver burrows into the riverbank to make its home.

Other signs of animals are their droppings, or scats, and tracks in mud or sand. Porcupines eat big patches of bark off pine trees, and a deer may rub velvet from its antlers onto a low tree trunk.

The Work Of Beavers

Beaver

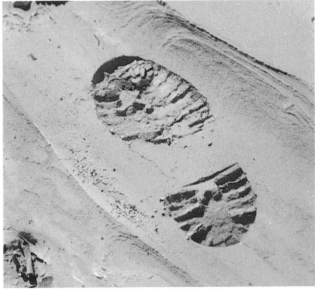

Animal Track?

Desert Bighorn

You won't find many signs of the desert bighorn sheep. Petroglyphs tell us the "ancient ones" may have hunted them over 800 years ago. Early settlers also told of seeing bighorns. These wild sheep lived in Zion until the 1950s. Then they seemed to disappear.

In the 1970s, park scientists tried to bring the desert bighorn back to one of its natural homes. They brought 12 of them to a big fenced area near the Visitor Center. These bighorns had young, and soon there were 20.

Some of the sheep were then moved by helicopter to a big area in the backcountry. A fence protected them from predators, other animals that might kill them for food. Park workers camped nearby to keep watch. After three weeks, the bighorns had made trails. They settled down in bedding sites they'd scooped out with their hoofs. It was time to take the fence away and leave the bighorn to survive on its own.

Maybe you will be lucky enough to see them scrambling over rocky ledges or drinking from springs in the side canyons.

Desert Bighorn Sheep ▶

Adapting Animals

Animals adapt to the area, or habitat, where they live. To survive, they behave in special ways, and their bodies adapt, or change. The desert bighorn travels in bands, always with one member on watch against predators, such as coyotes and bobcats. The bighorn's body can go without drinking water for days during cool weather.

Many of Zion's birds can share the same habitat when they don't compete for the same food. Different birds have beaks adapted for different kinds of food. A hummingbird's long, needlelike beak reaches deep into flowers to feed on insects and nectar. Flycatchers, swifts, and swallows can open their beaks very wide. As they dart through the air, they suck flying insects into their mouths.

Woodpeckers, nuthatches, and flickers use their long, strong beaks to hammer and chisel under tree bark for insects.

Seeds are easily cracked open by the fat, cone-shaped beaks of cardinals and grosbeaks.

When you go birdwatching at Zion, you can probably guess by the beak what each bird eats.

Hummingbird

Black-Headed Grosbeak

Hiking

You'll see more animals and many wild flowers if you hike Zion's trails. One of the most popular hikes is a hard climb to the top of Angels Landing. This trail is paved almost to the top. The last .8 kilometer is very steep, so there are railings and chains to hold as you climb. If you like high places, this is a wonderful spot to see Zion Canyon. Allow five hours for this hike which you can take alone or with a park naturalist.

Still higher are the trails to East and West Rims. You can hike East Rim Trail to Observation Point. The West Rim Trail leads to Lava Point where you can "see forever."

The Zion map lists all the hikes and tells how long they are. Get a copy of *Visitor Safety Tips.* Then be sure to take along your good trail manners: 1. If you stay on the trail, you are safer and so are the plants and wildlife. 2. Leave your pet at home where it's safer. 3. During your hike, leave nothing in Zion's wilderness and take out only pictures and memories.

e Organ — From Angels Landing

Other Hikes, Other Doings

For an easier hike, start with a stroll to Weeping Rock. You can pick up a booklet at the trailhead. It names the plants along the trail and tells how rocks weep.

Emerald Pools Trail takes you up to pools formed by two falls. This is a walk up a short way and back or a longer hike around a loop. You can hike it on your own or with a park naturalist who tells about plants, animals, geology, and history.

Gateway to the Narrows is an easy riverside trail to a narrow part of the canyon.

Wheelchairs and baby strollers are the only wheels allowed on Zion's trails. But if you like to cycle, you can go on two wheels along Zion Canyon Scenic Drive. Or if you can make it on one wheel, you can circle the campground on your own unicycle.

With all these things to do and places to go, you'd better leave time to relax. Find a patch of grass by Zion Lodge. Lie back and gaze at the blue sky over the huge Navajo Sandstone towers.

ving Arches—The Trail Down From Emerald Pool

ff-Highway Riding

Another Way To View Navajo Sandstone?

Beginnings and Endings

Take time to relax and think about the surprises you've found at Zion National Park.

Did you see the swamp beside the Gateway to the Narrows Trail? How about the yucca and other desert plants around Huber Wash? Maybe you saw layers of sediments collecting there as they have for ages in many parts of the world.

Who made the petroglyphs, and how did petrified wood form? What is a hoodoo and where is the West Temple?

Have you looked closely at the river where tadpoles are changing into canyon tree frogs? Did you watch the moon rising above eastern Zion towers?

Ask yourself questions, then puzzle them out yourself, because your own answers will be remembered.

As you lie on the grass and look at the sky above the Navajo Sandstone, you might ask one more question. "How many grains of sand and how many years did it take to make Zion National Park —and why?"

Mt. Moroni And Jacob Of The Three Patriarchs ▶

East of Zion is BRYCE CANYON NATIONAL PARK. Knobby rock formations stand here below the jagged edge of a Utah plateau.

Other National Parks in Utah

CAPITOL REEF NATIONAL PARK is a "jewel" of many-colored rock layers in south-central Utah. You can see part of this park by car. But the best ways to see it are on a four-wheel-drive tour or a carefully planned backpacking hike.

Two great rivers, the Colorado and the Green, meet in the heart of CANYONLANDS NATIONAL PARK. This park's sandstone arches, pinnacles, needles, and fins tell a story of ages of erosion and weathering.

ARCHES NATIONAL PARK is north of Canyonlands. Its red rocks have been eroded into windows, pinnacles, pedestals, and free-standing arches. They rise above a desert where many kinds of birds, rodents, and larger animals find food and shelter among pinyons, junipers, yucca, and cactus.

Bryce Canyon National Park

Capitol Reef National Park

Arches National Park

The Author and Illustrators

Wyoming-born Ruth Radlauer's love affair with national parks began in Yellowstone. During her younger years, she spent her summers in the Bighorn Mountains, in Yellowstone, or on Casper Mountain.

Ed and Ruth Radlauer, graduates of the University of California at Los Angeles, are authors of many books for young people. Along with their adult daughter and sons, they photograph and write about a wide variety of subjects ranging from monkeys to motorcycles.

The Radlauers live in California, where Ruth and Ed spend most of their time in the mountains near Los Angeles.